THE 7
SECRETS OF
HAPPINESS

THE 7 SECRETS OF HAPPINESS

A Reluctant Optimist's Journey

GYLES BRANDRETH

OPEN ROAD

INTEGRATED MEDIA

NEW YORK

Cover design by Mauricio Díaz

978-1-4804-7229-7

This edition published in 2014 by Open Road Integrated Media, Inc.
345 Hudson Street
New York, NY 10014
www.openroadmedia.com

Contents

THE 7 SECRETS OF HAPPINESS

Introduction

On 17 June 2013 I delivered the Baggs Memorial Lecture at the University of Birmingham.

Thomas Baggs, born in 1889, was a Birmingham University alumnus who went on to become a teacher, journalist and war correspondent for the *Daily Mail,* before pursuing a successful career in advertising and publicity for the American automobile industry. When he died in 1973, Mr Baggs bequeathed a substantial sum to the university to provide for an annual public lecture on the theme of 'Happiness—what it is and how it may be achieved by individuals as well as nations.'

Yehudi Menuhin, the virtuoso violinist, delivered the first lecture in 1976. Mine was the thirty-seventh. I spoke for an hour. There was an audience of 1,000-plus in the hall. The response was extraordinary—and not what I am used to.

Here is one tweet, from someone called Grace Surman:

'Fabulous lecture courtesy of Gyles Brandreth. Just marvellous, brilliant, wonderful, best thing I've ever heard, transformational . . .'

There were scores more—all along similar lines:

Danann Swanton: 'Attended the annual Happiness Lecture tonight, thought-provoking & inspiring talk by Gyles Brandreth.'

Judy Dyke: 'Excellent evening hearing Gyles Brandreth give the Happiness Lecture. Entertaining, amusing and he gave us the 7 Secrets of Happiness.'

It was these 7 Secrets of Happiness that caught the audience's attention. As I left the hall people asked me for a copy of the lecture—and a copy of the 'Secrets'. I had neither to give them.

That evening and over the next few days people began to tweet and re-tweet garbled versions of both.

That's when I realised that I needed to write this book.

I agreed to give the Baggs happiness lecture at Birmingham as the springboard for a one-man show I was taking to the Edinburgh Festival Fringe and then on a national and international tour. The stage show is called *Looking for happiness* and this, I suppose, is 'the book of the show'. But it's more than that: it is the culmination of a journey I have been on for about seventeen years—since my best friend died, in 1996, and I lost my seat in parliament, in 1997.

My stage show is both larky and serious. This book is more serious than larky. I am here to explore the nature of happiness—what it is and how you find it—and to share with you those 7 Secrets. There will be occasional asides, personal stories and anecdotes, but I hope they are relevant. On my journey looking for happiness I travelled far and wide and met some remarkable men and women, from the Pope's exorcist at the Vatican to Buddhist monks on the banks of the Mekong River in Cambodia. I even travelled to East Lothian in Scotland, to the birthplace of Samuel Smiles, the father of self-help books.

Memorably, in South Africa, at his home in Cape Town, I encountered Archbishop Desmond Tutu—a bundle of joy, a man whose very presence spreads happiness around him. In New York, the week before he died, I had lunch with Quentin Crisp. We met in the Bowery Bar, on the Lower East Side, for crab cakes and whisky, and for two hours I sat and gazed in wonder at a ninety-year-old man with mauve hair—the self-styled 'stately homo of England'—as he told me the secret of how to be happy. 'Remember that happiness is never out there,' he said, 'it's always in here.' As he looked at me with watery eyes, he cupped his delicate hands around his heart.

In Copenhagen I met the Queen of Denmark and sat with

her, alone in her study, as she told me what her father had told her about how to be a good monarch—and happy, too. In Dubai, in another royal palace, I sat with Sheikh Mohammed bin Raschid al Maktoum and his entire government (they sat on a series of sofas facing us) as the ruler of Dubai and prime minister of the United Arab Emirates gave me what he said he hoped would prove good advice for life: 'Begin when you are sure of yourself, and don't stop because someone else is unsure of you.'

It was closer to home, in Dublin, that I discovered the 7 Secrets of Happiness, with Dr Anthony Clare.

Anthony Clare (1942-2007) was a remarkable man, scholarly, amusing and wise. He was professor of psychiatry at Trinity College, Dublin, and medical director of St Patrick's Hospital, Ireland's first mental hospital. He held a doctorate in medicine, a master's degree in philosophy and was a fellow of the Royal College of Psychiatrists. He was best known, of course, for his series of perceptive radio interviews broadcast on BBC Radio 4: *In the Psychiatrist's Chair*.

Anthony Clare and I were planning to write a book together about happiness, but then he died. (There is quite a lot of death in the pages that follow, but don't let it get you down. As Shakespeare reminds us: All that lives must die, passing through nature to eternity.') This book includes all that I learnt from Anthony Clare and what I have discovered since.

And what are my credentials? They don't amount to much. I am a former European Monopoly Champion and the founder of the National Scrabble Championships. I have been interested in 'fun' and the importance of play and playfulness for a long time. I am a former chairman and now vice-president of the National Playing Fields Association—which is how I came to meet the Duke of Edinburgh. (There is a word of advice from him in here, too.) Play, sport and recreation contribute to happiness, for sure. So does entertainment. I have written 'cosy' murder mysteries—as Oscar Wilde said, 'There is nothing quite like an unexpected death for lifting the spirits.' I have produced plays. I have written about and appeared in pantomime. I have played Malvolio and Lady Bracknell in two of the English language's greatest comedies, *Twelfth Night* and *The Importance of Being Earnest*. In the 1980s, at TV-am, Britain's first commercial breakfast television channel, I wore brightly-coloured jumpers because the station's Australian boss, Bruce Gyngell, was convinced that having the presenters wearing sunny colours made the viewers feel sunny too.

At around that time, I founded the Teddy Bear Museum in Stratford-upon-Avon—which I hope brought happiness to some. Then in the 1990s, as a backbench MP, I introduced a private member's bill that became the 1994 Marriage Act and for the first time allowed civil weddings to be held in venues other than register offices. I know *that* brought happiness to many. (As we all know, a wedding day is almost always a happy one. It's what comes after that causes the problems.)

There is a case for saying that my family has been in the happiness business for generations. My forebears include Jeremiah Brandreth—in 1817 the last man in England to be beheaded for treason. He was a revolutionary, but a poor one, known at the time as 'the hopeless radical'. I see myself as 'the hopeful radical'. And my great-great-great-grandfather, Dr Benjamin Brandreth, went to America in the 1830s and made his fortune—manufacturing and selling Happy Pills. These were little vegetable pills and they cured *everything*. Whatever the ailment, Brandreth's Pills were the remedy. Dr Brandreth ended his days a multi-millionaire and a New York State Senator. He was also a pioneer of mass-market advertising. Thomas Baggs, of Birmingham University, would have admired him.

Baggs, incidentally, is a name with five letters—like Gyles. This may be significant. Oscar Wilde believed that you need just five letters in your name if you are to make a mark on the world. He gave OSCAR and WILDE as two examples and PLATO and JESUS and JUMBO as three more. (In New York, Oscar was introduced to Jumbo the Elephant by Benjamin Brandreth's friend and admirer, the circus owner, P T Barnum. The thought of Oscar Wilde meeting Jumbo the Elephant is a happy one, isn't it?)

Thank you for reading this book. I am dedicating it to my wife Michele, in this, the year that marks our fortieth wedding anniversary. She has given me all the profound sources of happiness in my life: our life together, our three children and our six grandchildren.

This has been a personal journey, but it has taken me some-where anyone can go. The secrets of happiness are available to all. Remembering them is simple. Mastering them is hard.

'Go to the edge, the voice said. No, they said, we will fall.
Go to the edge, the voice said. No, they said, we will be
pushed over. So they went . . . and they were pushed . . .
and they flew . . .'

Sheikh Mohammed bin Raschid al Maktoum

1:
LOOKING
FOR
HAPPINESS

What makes you happy?

According to the dictionary sitting on my desk, 'Happiness is a fortunate state expressing, or characterised by, content, well-being or pleasure.'

According to Charles M Schulz, the creator of Snoopy and the *Peanuts* cartoon strip: 'Happiness is a warm puppy.'

According to Denis Thatcher, husband of Britain's first woman prime minister, happiness was 'an English summer's evening, an open bottle of champagne and the lady in a reasonably contented frame of mind'.

According to Anthony Clare—I recorded him saying this: I am listening to his light, lilting, Irish voice as I write—happiness is 'mid-morning in Umbria, sitting in the Italian sunshine, and laid out on the table there's wine and cheese and tomatoes with oil dribbled over them, and with a few friends I'm talking about something like this—happiness—and, so long as the wine's drinkable and the cheese smells like cheese, frankly I don't care, I'm happy. The people are key. Having people around you who make you feel good and think you're good is important.'

In my head, and on tape, I have the voices of old friends. Hearing them makes me happy. And the sheep that graze at the bottom of my garden—they make me happy, too.

Each to his own.

What makes you happy?

There have been many surveys. I have conducted my own, talking to hundreds of people in different countries around the world. I simply asked the people I met, 'What makes you happy?' I tabulated their replies and these, from my observation, are the top ten triggers of happiness in our time:

1. Laughter

People like to laugh. Laughter brings joy. Laughter makes you happy.

Funny people, who may not be happy themselves, make others happy. I was a friend of the comic actor, Kenneth Williams, who could tell a funny story better than anyone and brought happiness to millions in *Round the Home*, *Beyond our Ken* and the *Carry On* films. Kenneth knew how to make people laugh, and loved to make people laugh, but he had not discovered the 7 Secrets of Happiness. Towards the end of his life, he had painted himself into an isolated corner, professionally and personally. Through his intemperate and petulant behaviour, he drove many of his friends away. He knew what he was doing, but somehow he could not stop himself. In the end, he died of a drug overdose, aged only sixty-two.

Kenneth was blessed with the gift of provoking laughter and laughter is contagious. Happily, in a crowd, laughter is more infectious than a cough, a sneeze or a yawn. And laughter is good for you. Laughter relieves physical tension—literally. Laughter can relax your muscles for up to forty-five minutes.

Laughter also triggers the release of endorphins, the body's naturally generated feel-good chemicals, opiate-like substances produced by the brain and pituitary gland that can both boost your mood and relieve pain—at least for a time. Famously, a conversation with Oscar Wilde could cure a toothache.

Laughter also improves the function of your blood cells and increases your blood flow. It helps protect your heart and, because it decreases stress hormones and increases immune cells, it improves your resistance to disease.

It seems that *Readers' Digest* got it right: laughter really is the best medicine.

2. Friends

Kenneth Williams introduced me to some of my favourite lines of poetry. They come from the Anglo-French writer and historian Hilaire Belloc's *Dedicatory Ode:*

From quiet homes and first beginning
Out to the undiscovered ends
There's nothing worth the wear of winning
But laughter and the love of friends.

Kenneth was a better friend to me than I was to him. It was thanks to him, for example, that I first appeared on *Countdown* and *Just a Minute*. I feel bad that, towards the end of his life, when he was looking for company, I wasn't there. (I didn't like his constant smoking; I didn't like him when he drank too much; I found him too demanding. Those are my excuses.)

According to evidence from around the world, collated for the World Happiness Database, under the direction of Ruut Veenhoven, emeritus professor of social conditions for human happiness at the Erasmus University in Rotterdam, you tend to be happier if you have close friendships, though your happiness does not increase with the number of friends you have.

The research from Rotterdam, and elsewhere, suggests that it is the quality and not the quantity of your friendships that counts.

I can vouch for that. Not long ago I was in Paris and went to visit Shakespeare & Co, the celebrated second-hand bookshop on the Left Bank. Browsing the shelves, I was quite excited to find a book of mine for sale there. It was one of my recently published Victorian murder mysteries. I picked it off the shelf and opened it and on the title page I read: 'To my dear friend Gordon, with admiration and much love, Gyles.' I had only given the bastard the book five days before! I bought it there and then, added a word to my inscription, 'with RENEWED admiration' and sent it back to him.

Yes, friends can make you happy, but choose them with care.

3. Music

There is amazing stuff going on now with imaging scanners, looking at centres of the brain that light up when people are feeling good, when they're listening to Mahler or Mozart or Madness—or to whatever (literally) turns them on. In the laboratory, with functional resonance imaging, we can actually measure that tingle up the spine.

According to research published in 2013 by the Montreal Neurological Institute and Hospital, areas of the reward centre of the brain—the part known as the *nucleus accumbens*—become active when people hear a piece of music that they like—and the more they like it, the more active the *nucleus accumbens* becomes. It is the same part of the brain that responds when we have sex or eat a favourite food.

The Canadian research also reveals that the *nucleus accumbens* doesn't work alone: it interacts with the auditory cortex, the area of the brain that stores information about the sounds and music we have been exposed to through our lives. The more a given piece of music rewards us—the happier it makes us feel—the greater the cross-talk between these regions of the brain. According to Dr Robert Zatorre, co-director of the International Laboratory for Brain, Music and Sound Research, 'This is interesting because music consists of a series of sounds that, when considered alone, have no inherent value, but when arranged together through patterns over time can act as a reward.'

We can like a new piece of music simply because we like it, and it can make us particularly happy because in our brain it triggers a recollection of past sensations of happiness.

Music can make us happy and when we are happy we sometimes express our happiness musically—whistling while we work or singing in the shower. And the happiest singers, apparently, sing in choirs. They are the healthiest, too. According to a 2013 research study from the University of Gothenburg, singing in a choir is as good for your heart-rate as a programme of breathing exercises in yoga.

4. Dancing

A number of biological systems are bound up with our feelings. I don't want to get bogged down in the science of it all (I was bottom of the class in chemistry, physics and biology at school), but I have to mention the role of the 'endogenous opioids' here. These are more opiate-like substances that we produce naturally inside us, and sometimes activities that we engage in can stimulate them. Cycling is one example. Stealing an illicit kiss is another. Dancing is a third.

We can get 'high' on dancing—and the music we are listening to as we dance (see above) can make us happy, too. Dancing on your own can make you happy. Depending on your dancing partner, dancing with someone can make you happier still.

For a brief while, I took ballroom dancing classes with my wife. I loved it, but our teacher gave up on us because, as the weeks went by, my skills did not improve. My enthusiasm didn't wane, but my performance did not alter. I simply loved the dancing for what it was: a playful hour with my wife—with supper at the local Indian restaurant afterwards.

I have been approached to appear on *Strictly Come Dancing* a couple of times, but I have said 'Thanks, but no thanks' because I know I have no natural sense of rhythm and, while the exercise would be good for my body, I feel the humiliation of early ejection from the competition would not be good for my spirit.

My friend Ann Widdecombe loved taking part in *Strictly Come Dancing* because it suited her personality (she is no dancer, but she has star quality—she's an extraordinary cross between Danny de Vito and Margaret Rutherford) and she really found it fun. *Carpe diem* is her maxim: she knows how to seize the day and live in the moment and when you are on the dance floor the rest of the (troublesome and troubling) world disappears. For my friend Russell Grant, entertainer and astrologer, taking part in *Strictly Come Dancing* changed his life. Through unhappiness, he had ballooned to twenty-seven stone in weight. He is now sixteen stone and happier than I have known him in thirty years. He found 'bliss' (his word) on the dance floor.

5. Sex

As Ann Widdecombe will tell you, you don't need sex to be happy. That said, almost everyone I talked to for my survey included sex as one of the top ten things that made them happy. 'Love' and 'falling in love', and variations on 'marriage', 'my fiancé' and 'my partner' featured in the top thirty, but not in the top ten.

Sex, of course, is good for you—and marginally more so if you are a man rather than a woman. A recent study shows that men who have sex more than twice a week have a lower risk of getting a heart attack than men who have sex less than once a month. Sex improves your cardiovascular health and promotes longevity. An orgasm releases a hormone called dehydroepiandrosterone—which enhances immunity, repairs tissue and keeps the skin healthy. Men who have at least two orgasms a week live longer than men who have sex just once every few weeks. What's more, regular sex increases the level of the immune-boosting antibody immunoglobulin A, which in turn makes your body better equipped to resist ailments like the common cold. After sex you sleep better and wake up slimmer. Half an hour of love-making burns off an average of eighty calories.

Notoriously, to avoid sex people are said to murmur to their partner, 'Not now, darling, I've got a headache'. Intriguingly, it turns out that sex itself can be a cure for a headache. Sex, it seems, is a natural painkiller. When you are about to have an orgasm, the level of the hormone oxytocin in your body increases five-fold. This is an endorphin that actively reduces aches and pains.

So sex is good for you and, though not essential to happiness (sex does not feature in the 7 Secrets), if you are having sex on a regular basis it should contribute to your happiness.

The quality and quantity of the sex you are getting makes a difference, no doubt, but, remarkably, how happy your sex life makes you feel is directly related to your perception of the sex lives of those around you. If you *think* that you are having a better sex life than the couple next door, you're happy.

According to the man behind the research in this field—Tim Wadsworth, associate professor of sociology at the University of Colorado Boulder—people reported steadily higher levels of happiness the more frequently they had sex, but those who believed they were having less sex than their peers were less happy than those who thought they were having the same amount or more.

All the research shows that sex within a sustained and loving relationship is what's best for health and happiness. A one-night stand can get the endogenous opiods going and produce a temporary high, but it won't bring lasting joy and may have you waking up pondering the power of Shakespeare's great line: 'The expense of spirit in a waste of shame is lust in action.'

For some, sex brings happiness. For others, it does quite the reverse. When I was much younger (and rather prettier) I worked with, and was propositioned by, one of my favourite comedians, the great Frankie Howerd. I later discovered that Frank (as he liked to be called) made a habit of exposing himself to married men. Max Bygraves, Bob Monkhouse, Griff Rhys-Jones, and scores more—with each of us, Frank went through exactly the same trouser-dropping routine. It never led anywhere, except to remorse on his part and a plea that we would not 'tell on him' to his long-suffering partner, Dennis.

Who was it who said, 'On life's long and rocky road I have found the penis to be a most unreliable compass'? It wasn't Frankie Howerd. It was either Jean-Paul Sartre or John Prescott.

6. Sunshine and birdsong

I was a little surprised to find birdsong featuring so high on the list of what makes people happy, but perhaps I should not have been.

Birdsong heralds the break of day and the arrival of spring. Migratory male birds reach their nesting grounds a week or two before the females arrive: they establish their territory and, in the early morning, with the coming of the dawn, they sing, both to assert their territorial rights and to attract the females of their species as they fly by. We mortals like the idea of a new day. It gives us hope. As Victor Hugo put it in *Les Miserables*: 'Even the darkest night will end and the sun will rise.'

Spring itself, daffodils in bloom, bluebell woods and new-born lambs also feature in the list of the fifty things that make us happy. Spring is the season of rebirth, renewal and hope—and we like that. Optimism is important to us.

In Britain, inevitably, 'the weather' features prominently in any survey of what makes people unhappy. By contrast, we love the sunshine because it brings us warmth and light and a simple sense of well-being and that all's right with the world. Man has worshipped sun gods for longer than any other deity.

When I went to visit Archbishop Desmond Tutu in Cape Town he took me into the garden at the back of his house to smell the flowers and watch the sun setting on Table Mountain. We had been talking about the nature of heaven.

'I wonder whether they have rum and coke in heaven?' he pondered. 'Maybe it's too mundane a pleasure, but I hope so— as a sundowner. Except, of course, the sun never goes down there.' He began to hoot with laughter. 'Oh, man, this Heaven is going to take some getting used to.'

We talked about Nelson Mandela, too. Famously, on 9 May, 1994, on the town hall balcony in Cape Town, Archbishop Tutu ushered in the new South Africa and presented his country's first freely elected president to a rapturous crowd: 'This is the day of liberation. This is the day of celebration. We of many cultures, languages and races are become one nation. We are the Rainbow People of God . . . I ask you: welcome our brand-new State President, out of the box, Nelson Mandela!'

'The sunshine shone that day,' chuckled Archbishop Tutu. He added, more seriously: 'Sunshine was *very* important to Nelson in prison, you know, very important.'

After I had visited the cell on Robben Island where Mandela had been imprisoned for so many years, I bought his autobiography and found this passage: 'I am fundamentally an optimist. Whether that comes from nature or nurture, I cannot say. Part of being optimistic is keeping one's head pointed toward the sun, one's feet moving forward. There were many dark moments when my faith in humanity was sorely tested, but I would not and could not give myself up to despair. That way lay defeat and death.'

7. Children

I think children are on the list in much the same way as bird-song and sunshine are. They represent hope. Show most people a photograph of a baby and they will smile. It is the natural response.

Children make us happy because (in the abstract, anyway) they are innocent and carefree and full of new life—as we once were. We are hopeful for them (and protective of them) and nostalgic for our younger selves (nostalgia is a powerful emotion, and mostly a positive one).

When I was with Desmond Tutu, archbishop, Nobel laureate, and one of the most celebrated and admired people of our time, I asked him, 'What has been the high point of your life on earth?'

He replied without hesitation: 'The most gorgeous moment would be when I became a father for the first time, on 14th April, 1956, when our only son, our Trevor, was born. I was so proud and so happy. It made me feel a little like God.'

The archbishop then paused and added slowly (it was the only time he was hesitant in our entire conversation), 'And, later, with the way Trevor has lived his life, taking the wrong turns and causing pain and anguish, I have learnt something of the impotence God feels as he watches his children making the wrong choices. Sometimes, in my own life as a father, I have felt very like God looking at us and thinking, "Whatever got me to create that lot?"'

Everywhere I turned in the archbishop's home, in the living room, the dining room, his study, alongside the trophies, medals, certificates and awards, I saw framed photographs of his family, dozens of them. 'What is Trevor doing now?' I asked him.

'He's some sort of consultant,' he said. 'He is a very gifted person, very charming, when he is sober. He destroys himself, or seems to want to destroy himself, when he drinks. He has been in trouble with the police . . . But there we are.'

He looked at me, and blinked away the tears.

I first met Elton John in London—by mistake. A December or two ago, my friend the Earl of Snowdon—photographer and sometime husband of the Queen's sister, Princess Margaret—took me out for lunch to his neighbourhood restaurant in Kensington. When we got to the place, the manager told us that we couldn't go in.

'I'm a regular,' protested Lord Snowdon.

'The restaurant is booked for a private party,' insisted the manager, politely.

Tony Snowdon is not a man who takes 'No' for an answer. His lordship swept the manager aside and marched in to the restaurant, pulling me behind him.

It turned out that Elton John had taken over the restaurant for his staff Christmas Party. We were not expected (let alone invited), but Sir Elton, with great grace, made us very welcome and found us crackers, party hats and places alongside his helicopter pilot, chauffeur, cook, gardener, book-keeper and accountant. It was a bizarre occasion, but it introduced me to Sir Elton who has since surprised himself—'utterly amazed' himself, he says—by finding the greatest happiness in his life through his children.

Elton John and his partner, David Furnish, have two little boys, Zachary and Elijah, and Sir Elton says, 'I love my children more than anything else. They have changed my life completely. They have brought me greater true happiness than anything I have ever known.' When the children start going to school, Elton is going to scale down his touring schedule so that he can be there when the boys get home. 'Having kids changes you. There is nothing more important in my life than my children.'

I am with Elton on this. All in all, I would say that my children—and my grandchildren—have been among the most consistent providers of pride, pleasure and happiness in my life.

But the John/Brandreth experience is not universal. According to evidence provided by the 20,000 and more users of the World Happiness Database in Rotterdam, having children lowers your happiness levels, but your happiness increases when they grow up and leave home. Children are a joy, but bringing them up is challenging, expensive and exhausting. Having a child ensures that you will be physically tired for the rest of your life.

8. Family

The American poet, Robert Frost, gave us the definition of home:

> Home is the place where, when you have to go there,
> They have to take you in.

Archbishop Tutu gave me his definition of the role of the family. 'I have a very strong weakness for being liked,' he confessed. 'I want to be popular. I love to be loved. One has enjoyed the limelight. I am guilty of the sin of pride. Sometimes I find it very difficult to be humble—that is why it is so good to have Leah, my wife. She pulls me down a peg or two. To her I'm not an archbishop with a Nobel prize: I'm just a not-very-good husband who likes gardens but won't do any gardening. Your family is there to do what your guardian angel is supposed to do: keep your ego manageable and remind you that you are just a man. "Thou art dust and to dust thou shalt return".'

Your family know you and you know them. They provide what another American poet called 'the security of known relationships'. When I was conducting my survey and asking people what made them happy, a lot of those I questioned, especially older people, said 'keeping in touch with your family'.

The most famous British family must be the Royal Family. They are not typical, I know[1], but they are a family all the same. The Queen, for example, likes to keep in touch with her family, but because she is Queen it isn't easy just to pop round to see the children and grandchildren when the mood takes her. That's why, so I am told, she spends a lot of time on the telephone. The Duke of Edinburgh once told me he couldn't believe how much time the Queen spent on the telephone. 'Simply extraordinary,' he said. (According to the latest figures, the Queen's telephone bill tops £200,000 per annum. It can't just be Her Majesty gossiping with her family, can it?)

Talking on the telephone is an established royal family tradition. When they were alive, the Queen, apparently, spoke with her sister and her mother on the phone most days. And the Queen's grandfather, King George V, chatted to his unmarried sister every day on the telephone. Once, Princess Victoria telephoned the King at Buckingham Palace and said, 'Is that you, you old fool?'—only to have the operator reply: 'Beg pardon, Your Royal Highness, His Majesty is not yet on the line.'

---

1   I do know it. When told by a friend (Joan Plowright the actress, the wife of Laurence Olivier) that her baby boy (Richard Olivier) had just spoken his first word (it was 'Dada'), Princess Margaret countered that her little boy (David, Viscount Linley) had just spoken *his* first word. 'And what was it?' asked Joan Plowright. 'Chandelier' replied the Queen's sister, proudly.

9. Drink and drugs

I don't drink. I haven't touched a drop of alcohol in more than ten years. Initially, I gave up drinking in order to lose weight. While I was an MP, I had piled on the pounds. Once I had achieved my target weight-loss (it took about four months to lose twenty pounds in all), I had a glass of wine to celebrate—and saw flashing lights in front of my eyes. I had become allergic to alcohol. My doctor says it's not that unusual among 'men of a certain age'. I don't miss the drink—not even that six o'clock sundowner. The upside is that, since I stopped drinking, I have not fallen asleep in front of the television once—and I used to all the time. The downside is that I want to leave the party just as everybody else seems to think it's warming up.

But this isn't about me, it's about *us*—and if *you* enjoy an occasional drink you will be pleased to know that almost all the research suggests that drinking in moderation (especially a nightly glass of red wine) is good for your health and your happiness. According to the World Happiness Database, people who drink in moderation are happier than people who do not drink at all.

I know nothing about recreational drugs. I have never tried them. In my entire life I have not smoked one single cigarette. (At school, I found other things to do behind the bike sheds.) I am not judgemental about this. I am just wary of artificial highs and I know that Hester Brandreth, the youngest of my three sisters, and rather a special person, would not have died aged sixty if it hadn't been for the drink and drugs she took on board in her younger days. (When she was older, she found a lifeline—and true happiness—through Alcoholics Anonymous.)

Drugs don't feature among the 7 Secrets of Happiness, though quite a few of those I spoke to during my researches mentioned drugs, their pleasures and their pitfalls. I met the Hollywood film actor, Richard Dreyfuss, star of *The Goodbye Girl, Jaws* and *Close Encounters of the Third Kind,* after he had given up drink and drugs. We had dinner together and he told me that he is 'quite comfortable' around alcohol nowadays. Others can drink and he won't crave it. 'But if there was a line of coke on this table right now,' he said, 'you would need six strong men to keep me from it. I would have to be dragged screaming into the street. I could not resist it. Coke is *wonderful.*'

You have been warned.

10. Food, in general; chocolate, in particular

Of course, food makes us happy. It is the stuff of life. Good food tastes good and does you good. And eat it in the right company in the right setting and you have a 'happiness scenario'. My wife and I enjoy nothing more than eating smoked salmon and cream cheese sandwiches, sitting side by side in the car in Richmond Park, watching the joggers and the deer go by. As we have seen, Anthony Clare loved wine and cheese with friends on a hillside in Umbria. Tony Snowdon prefers an intimate dinner party. His rule for a happy meal among friends is simple: 'No table too small, no ceiling too low.'

Mae West liked to say, 'Too much of a good thing is wonderful.' She was wrong, alas. Too much food makes you fat. Very fat people tend to be unhappy and obesity is a killer. That said, there is some evidence that moderately plump people are happier than very thin people. The bottom line is that research led by the Population Health Research Institute, which analysed 17,200 DNA samples from participants in twenty-one countries, found that the gene FTO, the major genetic contributor to obesity, is also associated with an eight per cent reduction in the risk of depression.

When I asked people what makes them happy, I got lots of answers featuring food, from the generic (ice cream/pasta) to the specific (including lobster mayonnaise, bacon butties and cookies-and-cream ice cream). The foodstuff that came out way ahead of all the rest, however, was chocolate.

As the philosopher and cartoonist Charles M Schulz put it so well: All you need is love. But a little chocolate now and then doesn't hurt.'

Chocolate makes us happy for all sorts of reasons. We know that dark chocolate is good for our health—in moderation. The cocoa content in dark chocolate provides antioxidants called flavonoids which are reckoned to counteract high blood pressure, promote cardiac health and prevent cancers. More to the point, chocolate contains a touch of tryptophan, the amino acid used by the brain to make serotonin, the neurotransmitter than can produce sensations of happiness. Chocolate also contains phenylethylalanine and theobromine: the one acts as an anti-depressant when it combines with the dopamine that is naturally present in the brain, and the other generates a 'high' similar to the caffeine rush that comes with a shot of strong coffee. (According to scientists at the Neurosciences Institute in San Diego, chocolate contains substances that produce a mild cannabis-like effect on the brain. The emphasis is on the mild. You would need to consume twenty-pounds of chocolate to generate the same sensation as a single 'joint'.)

The phenylethylalanine in chocolate also stimulates those sensations of attraction and nervous excitement associated with the initial euphoria of falling in love. Ah, yes, 'The Lady loves Milk Tray'—and for a reason.

When I gave the happiness lecture at Birmingham University I was welcomed to the platform by the university's chancellor, Sir Dominic Cadbury, whose forebear, John Cadbury, founded the Cadbury confectionary business in Bull Street, Birmingham, back in 1824. In 2013 Cadbury's conducted their own happiness survey of 2,000 people across the United Kingdom and came to the conclusion that the happiest person in the land is likely to be a sixty-year-old married teacher from Edinburgh called Steve. And he wears glasses.

The Cadbury's survey also found:

- The happiest people in Britain live in Edinburgh, Cardiff and Southampton; the unhappiest are living in Liverpool, Newcastle and Norwich.

- The happiest women in the UK are called Wendy, Lesley, Sandra, Anne and Mary; the unhappiest women are called Tina, Rebecca, Alison, Caroline and Emma.

- The happiest men are named Steve, Norman, Tom, Alan and Ken; the unhappiest men are named Gary, Chris, Mike, Mark and Ian.

According to Cadbury's, men are marginally happier than women and you are likely to be more contented if you have blue eyes, light-coloured hair and wear spectacles. What's more, people in their seventies are generally happier than people in their twenties.

This last finding chimes with my own experience. On the whole, while I resent the aches and pains of age, the middle-of-the-night trip to the bathroom, the horror of realising that I am beginning to look like a combination of my parents (not in their prime, but in their decrepitude) and that I am beginning to sound and act like them, too, I am surprised to find that, in other respects, I am quite happy getting older. It's good knowing that when the phone rings it's not for me.

Curiously, I am even quite happy with the prospect of death. Now that my children are grown up and the mortgage has been cleared, my business here is done, really. It'll be a bit of a relief not to have to struggle with life any more. I am not death-obsessed, but I am not frightened of dying (as I think I was when I was younger), largely because I have now seen so many people die—father, mother, sister, brother, friends of all sorts, from male best friend to first serious girlfriend—and all of them (except those killed in accidents) handled the advents of their deaths with extraordinary courage, grace and equanimity. In my experience, in a real crisis most people behave tremendously well.

Recently, I hosted the British Funeral Directors' Awards. (The first prize was for thinking outside the box.) After the rehearsal, I asked if I might try out one of the display coffins for size. It was a happy experience—genuinely so. I felt surprisingly comfortable, secure and at peace lying in the silk-lined casket, and when the lid was lowered over me I remained unperturbed. European Union regulations now require all coffins to come fitted with air-holes. Yes, if you are incarcerated by mistake, you will be able to breathe easy until the very moment your coffin hits the incinerator.

The history of happiness

Once upon a time, death was seen as the gateway to happiness. And not so long ago.

I was brought up in London and, as a child, I went to church several times a week. Church was central to my parents' way of life. My father was a churchwarden and taught Sunday school. To the end of his days, my father said his prayers every night on his knees at his bedside and my mother continued to send a 'tithe' to her local church long after she could afford it. At the beginning of the twentieth century, my father's grandfather dissipated much of his fortune—the Brandreth Pills fortune!—building chapels in North West England and North Wales, and my mother's mother became a missionary, travelling around India on a donkey with a bible. When I was a boy in London I sang in the choirs at Holy Trinity, Brompton, and

St Mary Abbot's, Kensington, and was a server at St Stephen's, Gloucester Road—one of those glorious Victorian churches that would make John Betjeman's heart skip a beat. At each of the churches I attended (and particularly at St Stephen's), and from my grandmother, I remember that life was regularly described as 'a vale of tears'.

For people of my grandmother's generation and perspective, happiness was not for this world. Indeed, the notion of happiness on earth was a delusion and a snare. Happiness was the state you would arrive at after you were dead—in that comforting coffin—if you did everything the right way. Happiness was a distant prospect: a promise for the hereafter, not a right for the here-and-now. Happiness was the reward on offer in the next world in return for the good behaviour delivered in this. Heaven was where you would find happiness—eventually. You might get a glimpse of heaven on earth, but nothing more.

When I came to talk about this with Dr Anthony Clare (brought up by good Catholic parents), he told me that in Ireland in the 1950s and 1960s, 'when the Irish Catholic Church was trying to come to terms with sexuality, some of the more complicated priests or nuns, who were supposed to know nothing about it, would assume that sexual ecstasy was a glimpse of heavenly happiness.'

In the Bible, in the Old Testament, we are introduced to the notion of 'the vale of tears' (a.k.a. 'the valley of misery', depending on the translation) in Psalm 84. In the New Testament, St John reminds us that ours is a world of 'travail and tribulation'. For thousands of years, misery and tears, tribulation and travail were what life had to offer, and happiness, as of right, was not in any sense on the agenda.

People experienced happiness, to be sure. There are some happy characters in the Bible—the beneficiaries of miracles, for example, the Good Samaritan and the Prodigal Son. (The Bible fails to record the famous last words of the Fatted Calf: 'I hear the young master has returned.') Chaucer has some happy pilgrims travelling to Canterbury. Shakespeare wrote as many comedies as tragedies. But for most people for most of the history of the world, from the days of the Plagues of Egypt, through the years of the Black Death to the time of the Dickensian workhouse and the Irish famine, life was a bitch and then you died.

'Happiness' as an English word has been around since at least the sixteenth century, but in its early usage it referred to 'happenstance'—good fortune. In medieval English, if you were 'happy' you had 'good hap': you were favoured by circumstance. Happiness was a matter of chance. It was not an expectation, let alone a right.

When did this change?

I think we can pin a date to it: 4 July 1776.

That is the day when the United States Declaration of Independence was adopted. Primarily drafted by the great Thomas Jefferson, it contained these sonorous words:

We hold these truths to be self-evident, that all men are created equal, that they are endowed by their Creator with certain unalienable Rights, that among these are Life, Liberty and the pursuit of Happiness.

Bingo! Yey! It's in the Constitution—as good as.

And now, we're all after it. We expect heaven on earth.

Of course, the 'Happiness' Jefferson had in mind in 1776 was not necessarily the kind of 'happiness' we are now after in the touchy-feely twenty-first century. Jefferson meant 'pursuing Happiness' as opposed to 'accepting Misery'.

Jefferson and the other founding fathers were familiar with the work of the Reverend Francis Hutcheson (1694-1746), Irish-born philosopher and one of the founding fathers of the Scottish enlightenment. It was Hutcheson who introduced the pursuit of happiness as a principle of moral and political action. He has long been a hero of mine because he was also the first philosopher to emphasise the importance of the sense of the ridiculous. Hutcheson came up with the notion that the fulfilled man should cultivate six senses in addition to the five (vision, hearing, smell, taste and touch) with which he is born. Hutcheson's essential extra senses were:

- a sense of self-awareness
- a sense of beauty

- a moral sense, 'by which we perceive virtue or vice, in ourselves or others'
- a sense of honour
- a sense of the ridiculous
- a sense of community, or *sensus communis,* 'a determination to be pleased with the happiness of others and to be uneasy at their misery'

Naturally, we would all like to see a world without misery, but when we talk about happiness today—and the happiness we are pursuing right now—it tends not to be Hutcheson's or Jefferson's general good that we have in mind. It's something closer to home: it is our personal happiness.

And the pursuit of our personal happiness brings us, of course, to Sigmund Freud.

Freud (1856-1939), the Austrian neurologist and founding father of psychoanalysis, is the man who really set the world about the business of contemplating its own navel.

And on the happiness front the great man was rather gloomy about our prospects. 'Our possibilities of happiness are already restricted by our constitution,' according to Freud. 'Unhappiness is much less difficult to experience. We are threatened with suffering from three directions: from our own body, which is doomed to decay and dissolution and which cannot even do without pain and anxiety as warning signals; from the external world, which may rage against us with overwhelming and merciless forces of destruction; and finally from our relations to other men. The suffering which comes from this last source is perhaps more painful to us than any other.'

Pass the cyanide pill, darling, it's just too depressing for words.

In a nutshell, in the Freudian tripartite model of the mind, the *id* is the primitive, animalistic, instinctual element, demanding immediate gratification ('I want to ravage my sister'), that wrestles with the *superego,* the part of the psyche concerned with ethical and moral conduct ('My conscience tells me it's wrong'), while the *ego,* representing the cognitive and perceptual processes that inform behaviour, settles the matter ('I'm not sure it's such a good idea, after all').

The arrival of psychoanalysis in the United States and what the Americans did with it is important in terms of the modern attitude to happiness. The Americans took Freud and adapted him to their own purpose. Like it or not, we now look at happiness the American way.

Anthony Clare explained it to me like this:

Freud was a European pessimist. He didn't see the warring *ego, id* and *superego* as being resolved. But the Americans, with their passion for self-perfection and their notion of perfection being achievable on earth, took Freud's theory and turned it into a therapy to make you happy. And the result is that now, along with our air-conditioned four-door car and our house and our couple of holidays a year and a reasonable standard of health, we all expect happiness too. We demand heaven on earth. All the psychological theories today assume some kind of maturing balance between emotion and perception and cognition and will and impulse control. To what end? Perfection. A mental state of perfection is happiness. And the psychoanalyst has become the secular priest who will take you to happiness.

What is happiness?

Let's agree on the kind of happiness we are looking for.

Remembering that the dictionary on my desk defines happiness as 'a fortunate state expressing, or characterized by, content, wellbeing or pleasure', we are not talking about straightforward 'pleasure', are we?

We are not talking about complicated pleasure, either. There are those who get their kicks out of *Fifty Shades of Grey*, no doubt, but here—if I may say so—we are after more than a gratifying 'happy hour'. We are looking for a happy life.

'Highs' come and go: they can give us moments of joy, excitement, satisfaction and delight—but they don't sustain us. They can amuse and distract us—they may add to our happiness—but, by definition, they don't last. We are looking for a happiness that is fundamental and enduring.

We are looking for a sense of well-being, aren't we? Not a sense of serenity (that sounds a bit otherworldly, po-faced and complacent), but a sense of completeness, balance and proportion, a sense of ease and content—as opposed to disease and discontent. A sense that things are as they should be—a sense that, with us, and within us, all is well, all is right.

I think that the essence of happiness is a conscious appreciation of the rightness of being.

The wellsprings of happiness

'The very purpose of our life is to seek happiness.'

Dalai Lama XIV

In 1960, a year before he died, Carl Jung, the Swiss psychotherapist and founder of analytical psychology, was asked to list the basic factors that make for happiness in the human mind. Based on the experience of a long life spent meeting, analysing and trying to understand people, this was the list he came up with:

1. Good physical and mental health.
2. Good personal and intimate relationships, such as those of marriage, the family, and friendships.
3. The faculty for perceiving beauty in art and nature.
4. Reasonable standards of living and satisfactory work.
5. A philosophic or religious point of view capable of coping successfully with the vicissitudes of life.

According to the Dalai Lama, 'If you have a particular faith or religion, that is good. But you can survive without it.'

Most of the happiest people I have met do have a faith to sustain them—be they Buddhists, Bahais, Sikhs, Muslims, Seventh Day Adventists or humdrum Anglicans. The Queen, supreme governor of the Church of England, is a supreme example. At 87, she seems very happy, driven by clear duty and sustained by simple faith. At 88, Gabriele Amorth, exorcist at the Holy See, is equally happy in his faith and in his work. 'I talk to the Devil every day,' he told me, grinning like a gargoyle. 'I talk to him in Latin. He answers in Italian. I have been wrestling with him, day in day out, for many years. It is hard work—physical work—but I rejoice in it.'

According to Jung, a religious faith is not essential to happiness, but some kind of philosophy of life is. It helps give meaning and coherence to your existence. And if it involves some element outside yourself—be it a set of political beliefs or, for those South Pacific Islanders in Vanuatu who worship him, the person of the Duke of Edinburgh—that's a good thing. It's not impossible, but inward-looking people have problems being wholly happy. We need resources outside of ourselves, according to Jung.

That's why Jung also thought education mattered. He didn't mean a narrow, scholastic education. He meant education in the sense of what he called 'an openness to knowledge'.

- - -

The original self-help book was called *Self-Help*. It was written by Samuel Smiles, a Scotsman from East Lothian who believed that the secret of self-improvement was self-education. He first outlined his philosophy in a speech in 1845: 'I would not have any one here think that, because I have mentioned individuals who have raised themselves by self-education from poverty to social eminence, and even wealth, these are the chief marks to be aimed at . . . *Knowledge* is of itself one of the highest enjoyments. The ignorant man passes through the world dead to all pleasures, save those of the senses . . . Every human being has a great mission to perform, noble faculties to cultivate, a vast destiny to accomplish. He should have the means of education, and of exerting freely all the powers of his godlike nature.'

Jung and Freud are the two giants of psychotherapy. Thanks to them the world is now awash with psychotherapists and counsellors. According to my friend Brett Kahr, leading Freudian psychologist, Winnicott Clinic Senior Research Fellow in Psychotherapy, and presenter of the BBC television series, *Making Slough Happy,* Freud is the single greatest social influence of the past century. 'Compared with the way in which our grandparents lived,' claims Brett Kahr, 'we, in the civilised world, take our emotional life more seriously, take childhood more seriously and are much more concerned with how each of us is feeling on the inside. That represents progress. The capacity for tolerance, compassion and concern between human beings is greater than it has ever been at any point in history and I believe that is as a direct result of the life and work of Sigmund Freud.'

According to Brett Kahr, even from beyond the grave Freud can help us all lead happier lives, regardless of our current state of mental health. Naturally, Kahr recommends Freudian psycho-analysis or psychotherapy (at rates in the UK ranging from £40 to £400 for each fifty-minute session): 'a private space where you can say whatever you want, without inhibition, restriction or betrayal.'

But this is a self-help book for people whose budgets may be limited, so here, as a prelude to the 7 Secrets of Happiness, are seven simple strategies, inspired by Freud's teaching, that, according to Brett Kahr, will help you live your life in a happier, more satisfying way.

1. Talk. Extensive research shows that people who talk are both physically and mentally healthier than people who keep their thoughts and feelings bottled up.

2. Make friends. Research suggests that most men would be hard-pressed to name someone (other than their spouse or partner) whom they could telephone with a problem at 2.00 am. We all have acquaintances: we all need friends, a small number of people whose inner lives we know about and with whom we are ready to share ours.

3. Keep a diary. Put your feelings into words. Texan psychologist James Pennebaker undertook an experiment with university students in which half of the subjects were required to keep a diary. Over a year, those who kept their diary regularly reported fewer illnesses and ailments, better mental health and higher grades in examinations.

4. Listen. People will be interested in you if you are interested in them. Listen to your friends and remember what they tell you. When you meet someone for only the second time and they remember your name, you always notice. Cultivate your hearing and your memory.

5. Cultivate intimacy. Most people who seek psychotherapy have difficulties in two arenas of their love-life: their capacity to relate intimately to their partner (trusting them and feeling comfortable with them) and their ability to enjoy their physical sexuality as fully as they might. Make time and create opportunities to talk with and listen to your partner intimately.

6. Be more playful: explore your fantasies. Many people at work (including the most successful) feel trapped in the wrong endeavour. Explore all your fantasies and develop the underdeveloped parts of yourself. Take your secret side-line desires seriously, but not impulsively. If you are a merchant banker who yearns to sing *Otello*, don't immediately give in your notice, but do consider joining the amateur operatic society.

7. Get in touch with your feelings. Develop your emotional literacy: allow yourself to take your feelings seriously or you will find they turn into symptoms (migraines, bad backs, etc). Overcome your embarrassment about your own emotions. Do not equate self-awareness with self-indulgence. It is good to rummage around inside your psyche.

Famously, Dr Freud said that the secret of happiness is 'to love and to work'.

In my life, I have been blessed with many opportunities to love. I have a wife, children, family and friends. I have been blessed, too, with rich and varied work opportunities.

My happiest working experience was when I was an MP and served in the government whips' office.

Essentially, the whips are parliament's Human Resources officers. They are also parliament's secret police. Our basic job is to get our MPs to vote in the right lobby—come what may. (The term 'whip' derives from the hunting field where the dogs need to be whipped in.) But to do our job well we need to understand our charges, their hopes and their ambitions. Each whip has around twenty-five to thirty individual MPs in his or her flock. To be in a position to persuade these MPs to do 'the right thing', to be able to apply appropriate pressure when it is necessary (and not when it's not), we need to know their strengths and their weak spots, and their secrets. I saved one MP from bankruptcy and at least three from scandalous exposure. They owed me their support. I supplied any number with a better office, a place on the committee of their choice, an invitation to a royal garden party, tea with the prime minister, a parliamentary trip to a sun-kissed island in the West Indies, the promise of preferment. They were in my debt. It was exciting work: the government at the time had a majority that ranged between nine and nil. It was satisfying work. I took it seriously and went beyond the call of duty. (My proudest hour came when one of the MPs in my charge died and I organised two funerals for him—one in his constituency, for his wife to attend, and another in Westminster, for his mistress.)

I loved the job because it was about people—and politics—but more about the former than the latter. I loved it, too, because of the close, closed, collegiate nature of the whips' office itself.

But it came to an end.

As Celia Johnson reminds us in the film, *Brief Encounter* (my favourite weepie): 'Nothing lasts really. Neither happiness nor despair. Not even life lasts very long.'

In 1997, I lost my seat in parliament. The people spoke—

and, in my case, in no uncertain terms. My wife wanted to put our house up for sale during the election campaign. She saw the way the wind was blowing. 'They don't like you, Gyles,' she said. 'They don't want you any more. Just face it and move on.'

There's no vapid optimism with my wife, I can tell you. When one door closes, it's shut.

I guess I don't take life very seriously. It's hard to get into this world and hard to get out of it. And what's in between doesn't make much sense. If that sounds pessimistic, let it stand. There's been too much vaporous optimism voiced about life and age.

Robert Frost

'Happiness in intelligent people is the rarest thing I know.'

Ernest Hemingway

Behind the complicated details of the world stand the simplicities: God is good, the grown-up man or woman knows the answer to every question, there is such a thing as truth, and justice is as measured and faultless as a clock. Our heroes are simple: they are brave, they tell the truth, they are good swordsmen and they are never in the long run really defeated. That is why no later books satisfy us like those which were read to us in childhood—for those promised a world of great simplicity of which we knew the rules, but the later books are complicated and contradictory with experience; they are formed out of our own disappointing memories.

Graham Greene

No vapid optimism

Life isn't easy.

Life is harsh. In fact, I'll say it again: 'Life's a bitch and then you die'.

Freud tells us that all we need for happiness is 'to love and to work'—and then what happens?

We read the small print and discover that Freud also teaches us that 'unhappiness is much less difficult to experience' than happiness.

Apart from death and taxes, and stroppy teenagers, there are no guarantees in life.

Work—you can lose your job.

Love—it can all go wrong.

Friendship—your friend takes your book to the second-hand bookshop within a week of you giving it to him. Or, worse, you have a real friend—and he dies.

In my stage show, *Looking for happiness,* I read out part of a letter that I wrote to my best friend—the actor Simon Cadell—a few years after he had died. I read it to illustrate the nature of friendship. I am reproducing it here now because I want to emphasise that the business we are about isn't trivial. It's profound. This small book you're holding may have a flower on the front cover and be called *The 7 Secrets of Happiness,* but what I am offering you isn't sentimental easy-peasy wishy-washy feel-good mumbo-jumbo. I know that life is tough—friends do die—and we want to be happy against the odds.

Dear Simon,

How are you? Stupid question, of course. You're dead. All the same, I wanted to write, to say hello and to try to work out why I still miss you as much as I do.

You'll be pleased to know that you have not been entirely forgotten by the wider public. Predictably, it's not for your stage work that they remember you. No, your immortality seems to rest on your portrayal of the holiday camp manager in the TV sit-com *Hi-de-Hi.* It could be worse. Sir John Gielgud had a late-life movie success in *Arthur,* and when he died one tabloid ran the headline: 'Dudley Moore's Butler Dead at 96'.

Because, Simon, for so long you were one of the masters of the voice-over you still crop up in unexpected places. The other morning I stepped out of the London Underground at Bank Station and, suddenly, over the loudspeaker system, I heard you booming at me: 'Mind the gap!' It's not much of a line, but I must say you do it brilliantly.

I stood on the station platform and let three trains come and go just to listen to you. It was good to hear that voice again (crisp, energetic, fruity, lived-in).

We met at school when I was fourteen and you were twelve. Why did our friendship work right from the start?

We had common interests and shared values, I suppose. We were equally self-absorbed, narcissistic, ambitious, but never in competition with one another. We were never critical of one another either. In time, our wives might tell us to spend less, drink less, improve our posture, hold our stomachs in, but we simply accepted each other, exactly as we were, without qualification, without question:

We didn't discuss our feelings, ever, not even when you were dying, possibly because we were middle-class Englishmen of a certain vintage, but perhaps, too, because, instinctively, each knew how the other felt and there really wasn't any need. We never had a cross word—not once in thirty-five years.

Our relationship was totally secure and wonderfully

uncomplicated. There was no jealousy, no envy, no confusing desire. That's the joy of friendship: sex never gets in the way. A love affair is fun, thrilling, (the highs so high), but it's unsettling, dangerous, exhausting too; and, if you've been around the block, you know it always ends in tears. Marriage (I think I understood this better than you) is magnificent—fundamental, essential, and, when it works, a blessing like none other—but it isn't easy. Living a lifetime with your lover/husband/wife calls for energy, staying power, infinite care, eternal compromise. Ours was an altogether easier lot. A friendship that begins in childhood is simply a favourite cardigan: you don't need to keep it in good repair, you simply need to slip it on.

We were good companions, you and I. We thought we were invincible and then, one day, we had our comeuppance. On the morning of Saturday 11 September 1993 I was standing in the kitchen at home, squeezing the breakfast orange juice, when the telephone rang. 'You are going to have to be brave,' you said. 'It's not good news. I'm riddled with cancer. It could be just a matter of days.'

In the event, you struggled on for two and a half years. You were funny to the last. A young nurse (she was very pretty) whipped back the bedclothes to give you an injection. 'Just a little prick,' she said. You looked at her indignantly: 'Darling, I'm dying, there's no need to be insulting.'

And now you're dead. And how am I? I'm okay. I lost my seat at the general election (a relief really). I'm back now doing radio, TV, journalism. I've lost weight. I drink less. It's fine. It's really very good. I want for nothing and I surround myself with famous, funny and delightful people. Oh yes, there's still laughter at my end of the table—but, old friend, let's face it: without you it isn't quite the same.

Yours ever, Gyles

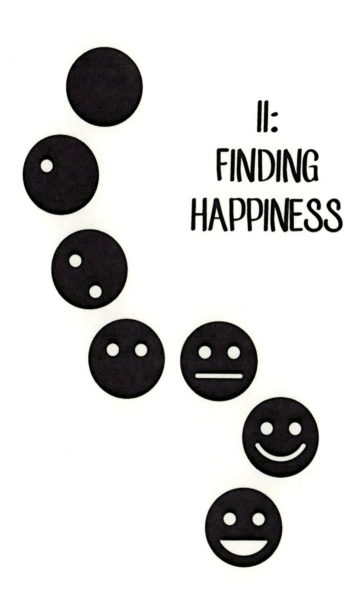

11:
FINDING
HAPPINESS

Finding the man
with the answers

It was around the time that I lost my friend—and then my seat in parliament—that I decided that I had to take this happiness business seriously.

If you knew me at the time, you probably thought that I was happy, almost irritatingly so. In those jumpers, on TV-am, on *Countdown* . . .

Well, I wasn't. At least, not entirely, not all of the time. I should have been happy, of course. I had everything a man could want: a lovely home, a good income, a perfect wife, three children who actually talked to me (that's the joy of money: it keeps you in touch with your children). I had it all, and yet . . . You know what I mean, don't you? Something was missing: something was wrong. I wasn't as happy as I ought to be.

So I went to see a psychiatrist.

Jung was dead. I knew that. I found a Freud in my phone book, but it turned out to be Clement Freud—not quite the same thing. So I decided to go and see the only other psychiatrist anyone in Britain seemed to have heard of at the time—the famous one off the radio, the one with the lilting Irish accent and the charming, disarming, penetrating way with him: Dr Anthony Clare.

I flew to Dublin to meet him. He was as delightful in person as he had seemed on the wireless. He was twinkly, amused, amusing, attractive, wiry and slight, beady-eyed, engaging: Gabriel Byrne meets Kermit the Frog.

He was at the top of his game and the height of his powers. He was medical director of St Patrick's Hospital in Dublin, Ireland's first mental hospital (founded by Jonathan Swift in 1757). To reach his office from the hospital reception I travelled through a labyrinth of corridors and stairwells, past sullen young women with eating disorders, past alcoholics and depressives, past shuffling figures muttering to themselves, past rows of old people sitting sadly in armchairs gazing vacantly into the middle distance. By the time I arrived at the great man's room I was feeling suitably shame-faced.

His welcome was wonderfully warm. 'And what are you after?'

'I am looking for the elixir of happiness.'

He laughed. 'If it's an elixir you're after, Dublin's not a bad place to start.'

'No,' I persisted, 'I'm serious. I want to be happy. I want to be happier. I want you to point me in the right direction. I want the 7 Secrets of Happiness. I want the rules.'

He laughed. 'There are seven secrets, are there?'

'I'm sure there are seven. There usually are.'

Anthony Clare was celebrated as a 'media shrink', but he was serious too. He was professor of clinical psychiatry at Trinity College, a research scientist and a scholar. He said, 'I'll help you if I can, but remember, psychiatrists are very much better at exploring the pathological and the diseased and the malfunctioning, so you've got to be wary of those who come to the issue of health from disease or come to the issue of happiness from mental illness.'

'I'll remember,' I said.

He poured coffee, invited me to take my place in the psychiatrist's chair, and suggested we might begin with a definition.

'What is happiness?'

There was a long pause. He was sitting behind his desk. He closed his eyes and screwed up his face. Eventually, eyes tight shut, he spoke.

'I pause because so many people talk about happiness as a physiological state—that's to say certain kinds of hormones are flowing around your system and, as a consequence, you feel a certain way—but others believe that isn't so much happiness as ecstasy, or some kind of elation.'

'And what's your definition of happiness?' I asked.

He opened his eyes. 'I would say happiness is a cognitive state, an intellectual perception or understanding of you, the person, and your relationship with your environment. It does have pleasurable components, but that's not the essence of happiness. The essence of happiness is a conscious appreciation of the rightness of being.'

He looked me in the eye, to make sure I was following. 'I am with you,' I said. 'I've made a note of that.'

'And it's a state,' he went on, 'It's not a permanent trait. People aren't "happy"—they have experiences of happiness. Most people's customary state is one of balance between conflicting needs and desires and emotions, and happiness comes into play as one of those experiences which people from time to time describe and clearly aim for.'

That day, and subsequently, Anthony Clare and I talked together about every aspect of happiness. I learnt a lot. Professor Clare taught me about the number of biological systems that are bound up with our feelings. He introduced me to the role of the endogenous opioids. These, as I have mentioned, are opiate-like substances that we produce inside us, and sometimes activities that we engage in can stimulate them—jogging for example, or some of the arousal jags that people put themselves into, climbing mountains, putting themselves in danger—clambering naked into hold-alls and zipping themselves inside. (People do strange things in pursuit of 'happiness'. Among four close friends of mine who died prematurely in the 1990s was

Stephen Milligan, MP. I had known him since we were at university together. Stephen and I had a happy lunch one Friday early in 1994 and then he went off home for the weekend, dressed himself up in stockings and suspenders and played a solo sex game involving a black plastic bag and a length of flex that went disastrously wrong and led to his death.)

'You do something that prompts a natural high,' explained Anthony Clare. 'It's almost as if you've got access to your own fix. And that's led to a lot of interest in the possibility that people who are prone to taking external substances—opiates, hallucinogens, amphetamines and so on—are people who, for one reason or another, have an internal opioid system that doesn't work very well, so they need external stimulation.'

It's fascinating and complex because while the biological systems may be a prerequisite to happiness—if your serotonin is low or your endogenous opioids are blunted, then it may indeed be difficult to feel happy—just because they are functioning well doesn't mean that you are going to be happy. 'As in every human feeling state,' explained my Irish guru, 'there is a number of components, all of which have to be present. You need a reasonably healthy functioning system and then circumstances of a cognitive kind, of a personal and inter-personal kind, that have meaning and that you pursue.'

Repeatedly, before getting down to the matter of the 7 Secrets, he put me to the test. And if Dr Clare and I were testing you now, dear reader, we would start by looking at your philosophy of life—is it positive or negative? Do you see the glass half-full or the glass half-empty? It doesn't mean that you can't be happy if you think life is an absolutely pointless exercise, but it doesn't help.

Next, we would ask you: what are you doing with your life? Freud, as we know, thought 'to love and to work' were the two key elements of happiness. So, what's your work? How do you feel about it? Is it satisfying? Do you feel you are making a contribution and that it's valued? And what about love? Do you love and are you loved?

Who gets to be happy and why

'The man who makes everything that leads to happiness depends upon himself, and not upon other men, has adopted the very best plan for living happily. This is the man of moderation, the man of manly character and of wisdom.'

Plato

Rich, poor, married, single, disabled or healthy—does what you are make a difference to how happy you can be?

I asked Anthony Clare some important questions.

Why do some people talk of the war as the happiest time of their life?

Among those who fought in the Second World War there was a comradeship. People who might otherwise have found it difficult to socialise were thrown in together. They had no choice. And there was a shared philosophy, a common purpose. The basic fighting man felt he was doing something worthwhile. And those engaged in the war were testing themselves. That seems to be rather important. Happy people are rarely sitting around. They are usually involved in some ongoing interchange with life. Of course, we're talking about people who survived the war, not those who were wounded or killed. And I'm not sure how many back home felt that way, other than those in the blitzed cities where again there was this comradeship.

During the deepest troubles in Northern Ireland, in the Shankhill and the Falls, while people might not have described themselves as happy, they certainly felt a bond, a sense of community. One of the things that was destroyed when the slums of Dublin were moved to the suburbs was that sense of comradeship, of being together. I don't glory in the tenements of the thirties, Sean O'Casey's tenements in the city here, but my God, they did produce a sense that people mattered to one another.

What about individual circumstances that are conducive to happiness? Is wealth important? Are the rich happier than the poor?

No, not necessarily. It has suited all sorts of people to equate material possessions with a state of happiness, because that keeps you pursuing them. But money and material things are a means to an end. I do not knock them. Often they free people. It is difficult in situations of struggle to be happy, but it doesn't follow that in situations of plenty you will be happy.

So winning the lottery won't make me happy?

Not of itself. Money is an enabler, but our society has got it horribly wrong and confuses the enabler with the end.

Is health important? Jung seemed to think it was.

It can be an important component, but not necessarily. You will find disabled people who describe themselves as happy, and people who have led terrible lives who, because of a philosophical view of life and of suffering, describe themselves as happy too.

Does appearance matter? Do good looks help?

Being reasonably attractive is a help. People come towards you, warm to you. But you can be too beautiful. Extremes are difficult for human beings to cope with. Marilyn Monroe wasn't very happy.

What about family circumstances?

It may be relevant where you come in a family. There's some evidence that first-borns, who get all the initial attention and love, are more contented, more confident. They may also be more conservative, less radical because they like the world as they see it. A second or third child is immediately in a more competitive and challenging situation, so there may be a tendency for first-borns to be happier.

This is now a politically incorrect thing to say, but, on the whole, it's better to have two parents than one. This is not meant as an attack on single parents and, of course, we all know plenty of one-parent families that are successful and two-parent families that are a disaster, but as a general rule two-parent families are more conducive to happiness.

What about marriage?

In essence, marriage is good for men; and can be, but is not necessarily, good for women. If you take the four categories—married men, single men, married women, single women—it does appear that married men are the happiest and single men are the unhappiest. With women it gets more complicated. For instance, married women with a poor level of education are unhappier than single women, but educated married women are relatively happy. Married men do badly when they're bereaved, very badly. They either quickly remarry or they die. All women think their husbands will marry again. Women just don't believe their men can function without the kinds of support that marriage can give them, and it seems they're right. Women cope with bereavement far better. There's no evidence of a higher mortality rate among women in the two or three years after bereavement, but there is with men.

Anthony Clare was married, with seven children. I am married, with three. Julian Fellowes, actor, scriptwriter and creator of *Downton Abbey,* is married, with one. I have known Julian, off and on, all my life. (He is the only Oscar-winner with whom I have shared a bath: we were both three at the time.) Julian says, 'The best advice I ever received was from my mother: "If you want to be happily married, marry a happy person." I am glad to say I took her at her word.'

To be happy, it seems, men need wives. I was struck by the opening paragraph from the *Daily Telegraph* obituary of Valerie Eliot, published on 12 November 2012: 'Valerie Eliot, who has died aged 86, married the poet T S Eliot in 1957, when he was 68, and by sheer uncomplicated adoration achieved the miraculous feat of making him happy.' Ah, so that's how it's done.

On the other hand, whether or not women need husbands is rather more debatable. This was the view of author, Dame Rebecca West: 'There is, of course, no reason for the existence of the male sex except that one sometimes needs help in moving the piano.'

When I met up with the ninety-year-old Quentin Crisp in New York he told me that he had come to the conclusion that, for happiness, the single life is best. 'I had no opinions about cohabitation until the last four or five years,' he explained, 'but recently I have become a kind of mail-order guru, and people come to see me and tell me their problems. And all the problems concern the person they live with, so to be happy you have to live alone.'

Why happiness is important

'You fall out of your mother's womb, you crawl across open country under fire, and drop into your grave.'

Quentin Crisp

Why is anybody happy?

The Irish playwright Bernard Shaw observed: 'People rarely admit to being happy.'

People are wary of saying they are happy—even if they are. Perhaps because it sounds like an invitation to fate. Or it sounds smug. Or it sounds insensitive.

The English writer, Aldous Huxley, in his novel *Chrome Yellow* has a character sound off about 'happy people' being 'stupid people', 'completely insensitive'. There's the noise and the screams and the roars of life out there, and the happy people just don't hear them. How can you be happy when you see on television what's happening in Syria? Or Somalia?

Well, how can you?

It was a question I put to Anthony Clare. The world is full of war, starvation and suffering. How can a sane and caring person be happy in such a world?

'It's difficult,' he answered, slowly. 'It is difficult . . . but perhaps looking for happiness is one of the ways in which we cope with the horror of the world.'

Dr Clare was a lapsed Catholic. 'I can't really believe in a God that can suddenly and haphazardly intervene during one moment of history, causing air crashes, genocide and famine,' he said. Dr Clare lost his faith in God, but not in people.

He told me of a conversation he had had with another psychiatrist, a Scotsman, R D Laing, author of *Knots* and *The Divided Self*. Like Anthony Clare, R D Laing died in France of a heart attack in his early sixties. 'R D Laing,' according to Anthony Clare, 'was a very suffering man in many ways, but he recognised that if you allow suffering to overwhelm you you're not going to be of any use to anybody. So perhaps this process of being happy has an evolutionary purpose. It allows you to do things, to move forward. If you were too ready to become—understandably—unhappy, you'd be paralysed.'

I am a friend of the actor David Haig. As I am writing this, he is preparing to play King Lear. David works all the time, not only because he has five children and, consequently, 'beaks to feed', but also because he has found that distraction is the route to contentment. 'If I'm not absorbed,' he says, 'I find it difficult not to see the world from a pretty bleak perspective. But if I am tired after a day's work, I am entirely at peace.'

Unhappiness can lead to depression and paralysis. 'Humankind cannot bear very much reality,' said T S Eliot. Happiness helps you bear as much as you can. Happiness keeps you sane. Happiness keeps you going. And, wait for it, the *happier* you are, the *longer* you will keep going and the *healthier* you will be.

- People who are unhappy in middle age are up to three times more likely to die than those with a happy outlook on life. Fact.

- Levels of happiness among the over-fifties have a significant influence on the onset of disability, walking speeds and the incidence of coronary heart disease. Fact.

- The link is irrespective of factors such as age, gender, ethnicity, wealth and education.

These are the 2013 findings of the English Longitudinal Study of Ageing—a study of more than 10,000 people's lives over a period of years. The work was undertaken by academics from University College, London, Manchester University, the Institute for Fiscal Studies and NatCen Social Research.

The bottom line is this: happy people live longer.

This is what the study tells us:

- Those who were recorded as having greater enjoyment of life were likely still to be alive nine to ten years later than were other participants.

- The difference between those who enjoyed life the most and those who enjoyed life the least was marked, with nearly three times more people dying in the lower enjoyment group.

Not only the quality of your life—but the very length of your life—depends on your happiness.

You need the 7 Secrets of Happiness. And you need them now.

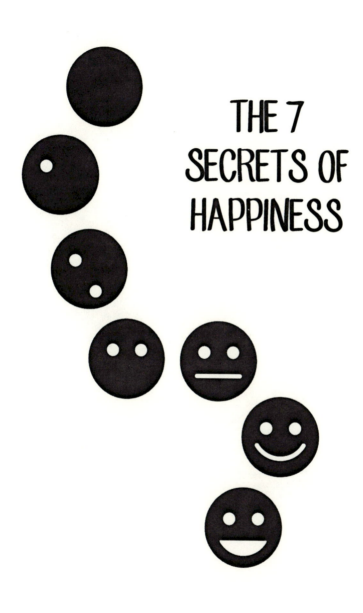

THE 7 SECRETS OF HAPPINESS

So here we are. At last. This is it. Read on: discover the secrets and follow the rules. They won't simply enhance your life: they will extend your life.

Initially, when I first challenged Anthony Clare to conjure up the 7 Secrets of Happiness, sitting in his office at St Patrick's Hospital in Dublin, we treated the exercise as a game (and playing games is good)—but as we talked the idea through, as we began to explore the possibilities and dig deeper, it became more than that.

Over the centuries many people have come up with good advice about how we can make our lives richer, happier and more worthwhile—and I notice, incidentally, that many of the best of those people have had five letters in their name. (Oscar Wilde, you will recall, believed that it was the five-letter folk who were most likely to make a lasting mark on the world.) We can learn much from Freud, Plato and Jesus, to be sure. In fact, we can learn so much from so many. The literature on happiness is vast. The worldwide web is awash with tips and lists and quotes, and 'happiness' downloads and self-help books and DVDs for sale. Look around and when it comes to advice on 'how to be happy', you will be spoilt for choice.

Given the welter of ideas and information out there—much of it interesting, much of it useful—we decided to rise to a particular challenge. We decided to produce, as concisely and clearly as we could, the essential distillation of what Anthony Clare had discovered through a lifetime of clinical experience and thoughtful reading, and so provide the *ultimate* guide, the *definitive* rule-book, the *one and only* easy-to-remember collection of principles and precepts that would mean that you would *need no other.*

Moses (another of the five-letter men) gave us the Ten Commandments. They have stood the test of time. Here now from Clare (and Gyles) are the 7 Secrets of Happiness—and the joy of the 7 Secrets is that they are—they really are—all you need.

You can read whatever else you want, you can sit at the feet of the god or guru of your choosing, but rich or poor, straight or gay, young or old, single, hitched or polygamous, with children or without, blessed with health or not, bald or beautiful, fat or thin, fun or tedious, whoever you are, whatever your circumstances, these secrets will bring you happiness, these rules will work for you. That's a promise. That's guaranteed.

The secrets are simple, as you will see—but living by the rules is not easy, as you will discover. If it was, people would have no problems being happy.

And you can't pick and choose. If you are going to live by the rules, you have to live by all of them.

1
Cultivate a passion

To be happy you must have something that you enjoy doing.

The challenge for a school is to find every child some kind of passion—something that will see them through the troughs.

The challenge for life is to find something that you enjoy doing—something that will sustain you, distract you, and delight you, when all else fails.

I was privileged to know Margaret Thatcher, Britain's first female prime minister, one of Britain's longest-serving prime ministers, and a remarkable individual by any standards. Politics was Margaret Thatcher's passion. Politics was Margaret Thatcher's life. And when she was ousted from Downing Street and lost her life in politics she had nothing—nothing at all—to fall back on.

I last saw her to talk to a few years ago when she was on holiday in South Africa and I happened to be there, too. Her husband Denis had died and she was lonely. She was visiting her son, Mark, but she was fretting that she wasn't in London. 'I need to be at Westminster,' she said, 'that's where I belong.' We talked about politics, of course—that's all she wanted to talk about, that's all she could talk about, really—but talking isn't the same as doing. 'I'm completely out of it now,' she said, with a sigh. 'Never mind.' But she did. She died on 8 April 2013, aged 87.

On 20 June 2013, another remarkable 87-year-old, Queen Elizabeth II, attended Royal Ascot races and saw her own horse, Estimate, win the Ascot Gold Cup. It was the first time a horse owned by the monarch had won the race in its 207-year history. 'To win the big one at Royal Ascot means so much to her,' said the Queen's grandson, Peter Phillips. 'This is her passion and her life and she's here every year and she strives to have winners.'

A senior man at British Airways told me how he had once escorted the Queen and the Duke of Edinburgh on a transatlantic long-haul flight and, after Prince Philip had enjoyed a session at the controls on the flight-deck, he had asked the Prince if the Queen might not also like to visit the flight-deck. 'Oh, no,' said Prince Philip, 'if it doesn't fart or eat hay she isn't interested.'

But if it does, she is. The photographs taken of the Queen at Royal Ascot as her horse won the Gold Cup showed a picture of pure happiness.

THE 7 SECRETS OF HAPPINESS

The other day, I happened to be with the singer, Rod Stewart, when he was given a model train as a present. Model railways are Rod's passion. To see his happy face light up with delight as he opened his present was positively heart-warming.

Building a model railway, breeding horses, singing in a choir, going to grand opera, playing Bridge or golf or bowls or Scrabble, ballroom dancing, stamp collecting, cooking, gardening, studying Wittgenstein, spotting UFOs . . . It doesn't matter what it is: cultivate a passion.

2

Be a leaf on a tree

To thrive, you have to be both an individual—you have to have a sense that you are unique and that you matter—and at the same time you need to be connected to a bigger organism: a family, a community, a hospital, a company, a club, a university, a school. You need to be part of something bigger than yourself.

Yes, a leaf off a tree is still unique and it has the advantage that it floats about a bit—it feels free—but it's disconnected and it dies.

The research shows that people who are best protected against certain physical diseases—cancer and heart disease, for example—in addition to doing all the other things they should do, are likely to be part of a community of some kind, are likely to be socially involved. If you ask them to enumerate the people that they feel close to and would connect and communicate with, those who name the most seem to be happiest and those who name the least are the unhappiest.

Of course, as Anthony Clare pointed out to me when we discussed this, there may be a circular argument here. If you are a rather complicated person, people may avoid you. If, on the other hand, you are a centre of good feeling, people will come to you.

Sitting with him at St Patrick's Hospital in Dublin, Dr Clare told me: 'I see the tragedy here in this consulting room where some people may sit in that chair and say they don't think they've got very many friends and they're quite isolated and unhappy, and the truth is they are so introspective they've become difficult to make friends with. Put them in a social group and they talk about themselves. It puts other people off.'

Sitting in Desmond Tutu's kitchen in his house in Cape Town, I asked him: 'What do you think Heaven will be like?'

The archbishop closed his eyes to ponder, and spread his palms out on the table. 'It will be spatially, temporally different,' he said. 'It is difficult for us to conceive an existence that is timeless, where you look at absolute beauty and goodness and you have no words. It is enough just to be there. You know how it is when you are sitting with someone you love and hours can go by in what seem like moments? Well, in Heaven, eternity itself will pass in a flash. In Heaven we will never tire. We will never be bored because there will always be such new sides of God that will be revealed to us.'

'And will there be people in heaven?' I asked.

He opened his eyes wide, looked directly at me and smiled happily. 'Oh, yes. Heaven is community. A solitary human being is a contradiction. In Africa we say that a person is a person through other persons. That's why God gave Adam that delectable creature, Eve.'

Think of the Garden of Eden and be a leaf on a tree.

3
Break the mirror

It won't bring you seven years bad luck. It will bring you seven to ten years of longer life. Break the mirror—stop looking at yourself—stop thinking about yourself—have done with narcissism and self-regard—avoid introspection.

A few years ago, I wrote an account of the life of the Duke of Edinburgh. While I was writing it, His Royal Highness allowed me to ask him anything I liked and if it was a 'matter of record' he would do his best to provide a detailed answer; if it was a matter of 'mere speculation' or if I was, in his phrase, 'hoping for a bit of colour to spice up your book' he would just look at me balefully and say nothing. Prince Philip does not like talking about himself. It is as simple as that. His youngest son, Prince Edward, summed it up when he said to me: 'My father plain and simply is very modest about himself and doesn't believe in talking about himself. One of his best pieces of advice he gives to everybody is talk about everything else, don't talk about yourself, nobody's interested in you.'

Nobody's interested in you. Get it?

NOBODY'S INTERESTED IN YOU. Understand?

NOBODY IS INTERESTED IN YOU! Point taken?

God may be. God is, according to Archbishop Tutu. But God is the exception and not the rule—and these 7 Secrets are for atheists and doubters as well as true believers.

Of course, your parents are interested in you (usually, if not always), but the odds are that they will die before you do. And your children are interested in you—to an extent. But, face it, they are much more interested in themselves. Once they leave home, they will try to remember your birthday; they will do their best to keep in touch; they will keep on coming at Christmas—for a while, until the time comes when they would rather do Christmas their way...

My friend Andrew Marr, journalist and broadcaster of quality and distinction, was caught out working too hard and kissing a colleague who wasn't his wife. Pressure at work, at home, and in his head, resulted in a stroke. He calls it 'a stroke of luck'. It has forced him to stop and take stock. He claims it has changed him and his attitude to life. 'I used to be so self-absorbed,' he says. 'My stroke's made me a nicer—and happier—person.'

Self-awareness is good: self-regard is fatal. Break the mirror. Introspection is a killer.

4
Don't resist change

Change is important. People who are fearful of change are rarely happy. We don't mean massive change, but enough to keep your life stimulated.

Change is the salt in the soup: change adds spice to life.

People are wary of change, particularly when things are going reasonably well because they don't want to rock the boat, but a little rocking can be good for you.

This, for me, is the most challenging of the 7 Secrets. Instinctively, I do resist change. I am a conservative Conservative. Politically, I like the old maxim: 'If it is not necessary to change, is necessary not to change.' On the whole I like things as they are. Or, better still, I like them *as they were.* (If a programme on TV doesn't seem any good, I fiddle with the contrast so that I can view it in black and white. I find that lifts the quality instantly.) I know that new technology is amazing, but, to be frank, I don't want to learn another frigging password. And as for those machines in the supermarket . . . "Unidentified object in bagging area" . . . Aaargh!

That said, I have done the research and seen the evidence and I accept that my instinct is wrong and that this rule is right. Remember those men and women in the Second World War bravely, boldly doing what they had never done before? As Dr Clare said, they were testing themselves: 'That seems to be rather important. Happy people are rarely sitting around. They are usually involved in some ongoing interchange with life.'

An ongoing interchange with life involves coping with change and embracing the new.

Uniformity is a tremendous threat to happiness, as are too much predictability and control and order.

You need variety in your life. You need flexibility in your approach to life. You need the unexpected, because it will challenge you.

Don't resist change. Go with it.

5
Audit your happiness

How much of each day are you spending doing something that doesn't make you happy?

Check it out and if more than half of what you're doing makes you unhappy, then change it.

Go on.

Listen to the psychiatrist, Dr Anthony Clare. He is addressing you directly from his consulting room. His message is to the point: 'Don't come in here and complain. People do, you know. They come and sit in that chair and tell me nothing is right. They say they don't like their family, they don't like their work, they don't like anything. I say, "Well, what are you going to do about it?"'

A recent study found an interesting link between time spent commuting and satisfaction with life. Perhaps not surprisingly, those who spent an hour or more on their journey to work were found to be significantly less happy than those who did not commute.

In 2011, the co-author of the study, Bruno Frey, in another paper, 'Happy People Live Longer', reported that happy people live fourteen per cent longer than unhappy people, increasing their longevity by seven-and-a-half to ten years.

This finding accords precisely with the 2013 findings of the English Longitudinal Study of Ageing and with research begun in Oxford, Ohio, USA, in the 1970s among the local inhabitants then aged fifty and over. Forty years on, in Oxford, Ohio, who has survived in good health? Those who had a positive outlook on their life and impending old age have lived, on average, 7.6 years longer than those with negative views.

Now, changing your job (or the place where you live) to reduce the time you spend commuting may be a difficult if not near-impossible undertaking, but, surely, if it helps add more than seven years to your life-span, it is at least worth considering?

Look at your life. Look at it carefully. Look at what you do and what you don't do. Assess exactly how you spend your time and how how you spend your time makes you feel. Audit your happiness and then, if you fancy living longer, do what you can actively to increase the happiness quotient in your life.

As one of my favourite actors, James Corden, puts it: 'The

difference between doing something and not doing something is doing something. So just do it. (Oh, and try not to take yourself too seriously. It's just not cool.)'

6
Live in the moment

The other day, I went back to my old prep school to give out the prizes. It was a happy trip down memory lane.

Before the prize-giving, drinks were served in the old headmaster's study. He had been an old headmaster, too. His name was Mr Stocks and when I was ten he was eighty. I can picture him clearly, but I can only remember one thing that he said to me. He said it to me so often I am not surprised it was something I could never forget. What he said was this: 'Keep that Latin accurate.'

He said it whenever he spoke to me—without fail. He said it in my report. I still have the picture postcard he sent me during the summer holidays. The message reads in full:

Keep that Latin accurate.

C L Stocks

Looking back now I think I understand the full import of Mr Stocks' message. At school, I wasn't that bad at Latin, but I wasn't as good as I could have been because I did not concentrate. I larked about. I told jokes. (*'In loco parentis* means my dad's an engine-driver'.) I made ink bombs. I looked out of the window. I did not concentrate on this lesson, because I was thinking about the next one, or about tea, or about choir practice . . . *Keep that Latin accurate*. Concentrate. Focus. Be present. Live in the here and now.

After the prize-giving, tea was served in the school dining room and there, carved into the wood panelling above the fireplace, was the famous line from one of the Odes of Horace:

Carpe diem, quam minimum credula postero

Happily, I have kept my Latin sufficiently accurate to tell you that translates, more or less, as: 'Seize the day, trusting as little as possible in the future.'

If you want to be happy, look at the things that you want to do and that you keep postponing. Postpone less of what you want to do, or what you think is worthwhile. Don't get hidebound by the day-to-day demands. Spend less time working on the family finances and more time working out what makes you happy. If going to the cinema is a pleasure, then do it. If going to the opera is a pain, then don't do it. And whatever you are doing, do it to the full.

And even if what you are doing is not wholly what you'd like to be doing, be wholly engaged in it nonetheless. When I visited the Queen of Denmark at her palace in Copenhagen, she said to me, 'Being Queen involves a lot of repetition—the same ceremonies, the same functions, the same routine, every year. Sometimes you think, "Here we go again!", but my parents taught me something useful that I have tried to pass on to my two boys. Whatever you are doing, be aware of it and stay involved. For example, I have to listen to a lot of boring speeches, but I have discovered there is nothing so boring as not listening to a boring speech. If you listen carefully, the speech is very rarely as boring as you thought it was going to be. You can disagree with the speech in your head. You can think, "He's saying it very badly," but don't switch off. Somehow listen. It is much better that way.'

Don't switch off. Stay engaged. Resist distraction. Concentrate. Focus. Be present. Smell the coffee. Taste the food. Listen to the speech. Keep that Latin accurate. Stop thinking about what's coming next, stop checking the mobile, and relish what's happening *now*.

Seize the day. For all you know, it's the only one you've got. Live in the moment.

'Try to learn to breathe deeply, really to taste food when you eat, and when you sleep really to sleep. Try as much as possible to be wholly alive with all your might, and when you laugh, laugh like hell. And when you get angry, get good and angry. Try to be alive. You will be dead soon enough.'

William Saroyan

7
Be happy

And, finally, if you want to be happy . . . *Be Happy*.

Act it, play the part, put on a happy face.

Start thinking differently. 'Choose to be optimistic,' says the Dalai Lama. 'It feels better.'

If you are feeling negative, simply say to yourself, 'I am going to be positive', and that, in itself, can trigger a change in how you feel.

That's it.

And it works.

It really does, I'm happy to say.

About the Author

Gyles Brandreth is a writer, broadcaster, and former member of Parliament and government whip, best known these days as a reporter on BBC1's *The One Show* and a regular on Radio 4's *Just a Minute*. On stage, he has appeared as Malvolio, Lady Bracknell, and in his own musical revue in London's West End. On TV, he has featured in *Have I Got News for You*, *QI*, *Ten O'Clock Live*, *Countdown*, and *This Is Your Life*. His novels include six Victorian murder mysteries featuring Oscar Wilde as his detective, and he has published two volumes of diaries and two royal biographies. He is married to writer and publisher Michele Brown and has three children, six grandchildren, and two cats.

OPEN ROAD
INTEGRATED MEDIA

Open Road Integrated Media is a digital publisher and multimedia content company. Open Road creates connections between authors and their audiences by marketing its ebooks through a new proprietary online platform, which uses premium video content and social media.

CPSIA information can be obtained at www.ICGtesting.com
Printed in the USA
LVOW05s1102220614

391137LV00007B/592/P